GREGOR

365

WAYS TO BE
Romantic
One For Each Day
Of The Year

MILLS & BOON

'365 Ways To Be Romantic' is an adaptation from
'1001 Ways To Be Romantic'
published by Casablanca Press™ Inc.

First published in Great Britain 1995
by Harlequin Mills & Boon Limited

ISBN 0 263 79100 9

Printed in Great Britain
56/9501

About the Author

Gregory J.P. Godek is a writer, professional speaker, husband and incurable romantic. He was romantic by inclination long before it became an avocation, then preoccupation – and finally – occupation. Greg has been teaching a class *1001 Ways To Be Romantic* for ten years at the Boston Center for Adult Education, and delivering keynote talks, seminars and workshops for a variety of organizations.

Greg once said that the world doesn't need yet another advice book offering the latest psychological cure-all. What people do need – and keep asking for – is a return to the basics: in this case, Good Old-Fashioned Romance. What people need is a practical book filled with specific ideas – because they don't need to be coddled, they need a handy reference and (occasionally) a good swift kick-in-the-pants. This book is both.

This book is for everyone who wants to bring more joy, happiness, peace, fun and passion into their lives. Greg isn't so bold as to believe that romance is THE answer, but suggests that it is ONE OF the answers. It is his Way. (And, yes . . . his wife says that he really does practise what he preaches.)

Contents

INTRODUCTION

Romance is a state of mind. If you have the right attitude, you can make cleaning the bathroom romantic; if you have the *wrong* attitude, you can turn a moonlit stroll on the beach into a fight.

Romance is about the little things. It's much more about the small gestures – the little ways of making daily life with your lover a bit more special – than it is about extravagant, expensive gestures. (Although the outrageous certainly has its place in the romantic's repertoire.)

There are *two* kinds of romance: **obligatory** and **optional romance.** Both are important, and although my focus is on *optional* romance, beginners are advised to be careful not to overlook the obligatory. But make no mistake about it: *optional romance is more genuinely romantic.*

Obligatory romance includes: celebrating her birthday; getting her a gift for Christmas; acknowledging your anniversary; remembering Valentine's Day.

Optional romance includes: *everything else.* Little surprises. Big surprises. Candlelit dinners. Champagne toasts. Weekend get-aways. Sending funny greeting cards, romantic cards. Surprise "dates". Romantic films. Love letters.

Why be romantic? Why bother? Simple. *It will improve the quality of your life.*

Romance is not gender-specific. Nearly every idea in this book applies to *both* men and women, even though I sometimes say "her" and other times "his". Don't forget that deep down, we all want the same things in life. Men and women have different styles – not different needs.

Listen! With your ears, mind and heart. Listen for the meaning behind his actions. Listen for the message behind her words.

Being romantic *occasionally* is one thing, but *living a romantic life requires consistency of effort.* Making romantic gestures is watering the flower of your relationship. Don't let it wilt!

Some strategies for being more romantic:

- ❤ "Tune-in" to romantic opportunities. They're all around you!

- ❤ Overdo something. Does he love **m&m**'s? Buy him 50 pounds!!

- ❤ Surprises. Big and small. Serious and silly. Expensive and cheap.

- ❤ Start with the basics, then *give 'em a twist!*

Romance is the expression of love. It's not the same as *love*, but it's the *language of love.*

Five Tips That Will Change Your Life

Romance is a balance of two concepts:

1. Actions speak louder than words.
2. It's the thought that counts.

These concepts are two sides of the same coin. Think about it.

Turn the ordinary into the special. You can make everyday events into "little celebrations" – opportunities to express your love for your partner. We're not talking *passion* here, but *affection*. A tiny bit of forethought can turn the ordinary into the special. Eat dinner by candlelight. Tie a ribbon around a cup of bedtime tea. Pop your own popcorn while watching a video at home.

*Understand the difference between a **gift** and a **present**.*

❤ A present is something you're giving the receiver because it's something **you** want him or her to have.

❤ A *gift* is something that you know the **receiver wants**.

*Let other things speak **for** you.* You don't have to be eloquent in order to be romantic. You don't have to write great poetry or even mediocre love letters.

❤ Let these people speak for you: William Shakespeare, Billy Joel, Paul McCartney, Charlie Brown, Susan Polis Schutz, Elizabeth Barrett Browning, Kahlil Gibran.

❤ Let these things speak for you: flowers, soft toys,

greeting cards, songs, comic strips, newspaper headlines.

Remember: Romance isn't barter! You'll lose every time if you use romantic gestures to barter for favours or forgiveness. The following "unspoken agreements" may have had some validity in the past, but in the 1990s they don't stand up anymore:

- ♥ I'll take you to a movie and dinner if you'll sleep with me.
- ♥ I'll cook dinner for you if you'll let me nag you.
- ♥ I'll give you flowers if you'll forgive me for being insensitive.

Romance is the expression of your love for that special person. It's not a bargaining chip. When you use it as one, you cheapen the gesture and devalue your relationship.

Classic Romance

1

Make a toast to one another every time you hold a wine glass. Make eye contact. Take turns making the toast. Whisper it.

2

Revive chivalry. Women love a real Gentleman.

- ❤ Open her car door. Hold her dinner chair. Help her on with her coat.
- ❤ Many women will love the revival of manners.
- ❤ Some women will need to be reassured that these gestures are tokens of respect and affection, and not messages that men feel women are inferior and helpless.

3

Go out dancing!

4

What could be more classic than a fine gold locket with your photo inside?

5

Serenade her. Sing her favourite love song, or "your song" to her. You don't need to have a great voice. Your sincerity will more than make up for your lack of perfect pitch.

6

A true classic is the lazy-Sunday-afternoon drive or a boat ride along the river. Dress in your Sunday best, pack a picnic lunch, and enjoy!

7

❤ Write a love letter! ❤ Pen a poem!
❤ Compose a song!

8

Rent some classic films!

- ❤ Casablanca
- ❤ Gone with the Wind
- ❤ The Philadelphia Story
- ❤ Singin' in the Rain
- ❤ Lawrence of Arabia
- ❤ West Side Story
- ❤ Romeo and Juliet
- ❤ A Streetcar Named Desire
- ❤ Doctor Zhivago

Be prepared!

9

Be prepared for spontaneous romantic escapes! Have "His" and "Hers" overnight bags packed at all times. Keep under the bed or in the car boot.

10

Go out this weekend and buy £20 worth of greeting cards. Don't ask questions, just do it! Head for your nearest card shop and spend a solid hour reading hundreds of cards. Find sexy cards. Get *several* birthday cards. Choose piles of friendship cards. Get some sentimental ones. Don't forget cards with no inscription, so you can exercise your creativity. Now you'll be prepared for anything!

11

Be prepared for shopping! Know *all* of your partner's sizes! You should be able to buy *any* item of clothing for him or her, and have it fit 80% of the time.

✳ Could you buy her *any* item of lingerie?
✳ Could you buy him a hat? A pair of shoes?

12

Be prepared with a music library of romantic albums.

13

Mark all significant dates in your diary. (Birthdays, anniversaries, Valentine's Day, other personally-significant days . . .) Then, write in reminders to send cards or buy gifts *at least one week in advance of the upcoming date!*

14

Make a list of at least ten things you *know* she'd love. Don't put this off till later – *do it right now!*

15–21

Be prepared – for anything! Always have on hand:

* A bottle of champagne
* A few candles
* A fun, silly and/or cheap "Trinket Gift"
* A serious/romantic greeting card
* A funny/romantic greeting card
* A nice lingerie gift
* An album or CD of special or romantic music

22

Write "Romantic Reminders" on your "To Do" list at work. Romantic Reminders will remind you that there's another part of your life that's quite important.

23

Be prepared to giftwrap your gifts. (Reminder for guys especially: the presentation is nearly as important as the gift itself.) Thus, have wrapping paper, bows, ribbon and boxes around at all times.

Be Creative!

24

Make your own greeting cards. Hallmark cards are fine – I have a drawer full of them – but home-made cards are extra special. You don't have to be artistic, just heartfelt. (Remember, she's with you not because you're Picasso, but because you're *you*.)

25

Hiding places for notes and small gifts:

* Under the pillow
* In the glove compartment
* In the bathroom cabinet
* In the refrigerator
* In his briefcase
* In her handbag
* In a pizza box
* Under his dinner plate

26

Make a "Commemorative Scroll" to celebrate his birthday, your anniversary, or any special year. Pick the year. Research the major happenings of that year. Write it up, type it up and present it!

27

Is she a crossword fanatic? Create a custom crossword puzzle. Make the clues reminiscent of your relationship and life together, include private jokes, funny phrases and names of favourite songs.

28

Make him work for his next gift! Leave written clues that lead him on a wild goose chase around the house, through the garden, to the neighbours or around town.

29

Make a "Mission Impossible" tape.

* "Your assignment, should you choose to accept it . . . is to meet a handsome, dark-haired stranger for a romantic dinner at the Posh Café, tomorrow evening at 7:00 p.m. I suggest you take on the role of a mysterious and ravishing beauty . . ."

* Leave the cassette tape in a Walkman with a note, "Play me".

30

Create "theme" gifts and presentations. Combine similar items and ideas to create fun, meaningful gifts.

Flowers

31

99% of all women *love* flowers. (The other 1% is either allergic to them or so practical that they'd rather have the cash.)

Flowers are great not only because they're appreciated, but because they're easy to order by phone; because flower shops grow conveniently on every corner; and because flowers come in every price range.

* Bring home a bouquet
* Give her one red rose
* Select her favourite flower

32
(Men like flowers, too.)

33
Bring home one flower a day. You'll build a wonderfully diverse bouquet day by day. It gives both of you something to look forward to, and you'll have an ever-changing, always fresh reminder of your love.

34
Place a flower under the windscreen wiper of his car.

35
Buy her a beautiful crystal vase (or a bud vase, if you're on a budget). Not only does it make a great gift, but it will encourage both of you to brighten up your lives with flowers more often.

36
Place a flower on her pillow. Just because.

Reprinted with special permission of King Features Syndicate, Inc. © 1978

37

Place a flower in his briefcase.

38

Did you know . . . that different coloured roses have different meanings?

Red = **PASSION!**
Pink = Friendship
Yellow = **RESPECT**
White = Purity

39

Send a special note along with special flowers:

✻ Tulip: "I've got 'two-lips' waiting for you."

✻ Sunflower: "You brighten my life."

✻ Forget-me-not: "Forget-me-not."

40

Send *one rose.* The power of simplicity. (The note: "This bud's for you!")

41

Your favourite flowers aren't necessarily the most fragrant ones. Create a bouquet of fragrant flowers and you'll fill the entire house with an aromatic reminder of your love.

Chocolate

42

Chocolate! There's just something about it, isn't there?! While I firmly believe that romance shouldn't be used as a bribe to curry favours, a box of great chocolates is an incredibly well-received gift, isn't it?

43

Reliable sources report that chocolate may *just really be* an aphrodisiac.

* Fact: chocolate contains large amounts of phenylethylamine, a chemical that is also naturally produced by the body when one has feelings of love.

* Observation: 99% of all women love chocolate. 50% of them *love* chocolate. And 25% of them *really love* chocolate.

* Fact: the Aztecs considered chocolate to be so powerful a stimulant that women were forbidden from having it!

44–45

Here are some travel suggestions for fanatics:

* Are Swiss chocolates the best in the world? To find out, visit the Nestlé Chocolate factory in Broc. Write or call for reservations: Nestlé S.A., Service des Visites, 1636 Broc FR, Switzerland; (41) 296-5151.

* The "Cadbury World Chocolate Experience" is in Birmingham, England. Cadbury has an exhibit on the *history* of chocolate (which features a taste of a chocolate drink made from an ancient Aztec recipe). Write or call for reservations: Cadbury World, Reservations, Linden Road, Bourneville, South Birmingham B30 2LD; 021-451 4159.

A Touch of Class

46

Hire a pianist to play during dinner at home.

47

Have his portrait painted from a photograph.

48

Propose a toast to her while at a dinner party with good friends.

49

When's the last time you visited your local art gallery? Museum? Planetarium? Public garden?

50

When's the last time you attended the symphony? The ballet? The opera? A jazz concert?

51

Hire a limousine for an elegant evening out.

52

Wear a tuxedo home from work. (Women *love* men in dinner jackets.)

53

Bring home a bottle of Dom Perignon. Celebrate tonight, or save it for a special occasion. (Just having a bottle of it around adds a touch of class to your house.)

Surprise!

Surprises are an integral part of the romantic lifestyle. The everyday and ordinary can be made into the unexpected and special.

54

The surprise get-away weekend is a romantic classic. Take advantage of near-by hotels' special weekend packages; or find a quaint bed-and-breakfast or picturesque inn. Pack bags for both of you, and whisk your partner away upon his or her arrival from work!

55

Send a taxi to pick him up after work; pre-pay the cab fare (including tip!), and instruct the driver to take him to your favourite restaurant, where you'll be waiting for him!

56

Buy tickets well in advance to the theatre, symphony or concert. Don't tell her what the tickets are for . . . simply tell her to mark her calendar. The mystery surrounding the event will be almost as much fun as the event itself. Guaranteed.

57–61

➤ Surprise her by bringing dinner home from a gourmet take-away café.

➤ . . . Or with a Big Mac from McDonald's.

➤ Surprise him with an *unexpected* three-day weekend. (Arrange it ahead of time with his boss and his secretary.)

➤ Surprise him with a "Trinket Gift".

➤ Surprise her with the latest novel by her favourite author.

62

If she's a one-of-a-kind woman, why not present her with a one-of-a-kind piece of jewellery? Check the Yellow Pages under "Jewellers".

63

While out shopping with her: if she's trying on an outfit she adores (or you find sexy) – pay for it quickly while she's still in the dressing room. (A good reason to carry cash on these little outings.) Return to the dressing room with a pair of scissors, cut off the price tags, and announce that she can wear the outfit out of the store. Watch her jaw drop. Then watch her leap into your arms.

64

Surprise Strategy #1: *The Time-Delay Tactic:* learn what she likes/wants. Get it for her, but hold on to it for a few weeks or months and surprise her with it when she least expects it.

Happy Birthday!

65

➢ Send 20 cards to her on her 20th birthday.
➢ Send 30 red roses to him on his 30th birthday.
➢ Send 40 balloons to her on her 40th birthday.
➢ Send 50 home-made cards to him on his 50th birthday.
➢ Send 60 stuffed animals to her on her 60th birthday.
➢ Send 70 sunflowers to him on his 70th birthday.

66

Send her a birthday card *every day for a month!*

67

Declare it your lover's *"Birthday Month"*, and do something special every day for the 30 days preceding THE day.

68

➤ Send him one birthday card for each year of his age – *one-a-day for as long as it takes,* or *all at once!*

69

And if you're not satisfied with celebrating once a year, you can always celebrate *half-birthdays* every six months!

70

Use sparklers instead of candles on his birthday cake.

"What a coincidence! You forgot my birthday and I forgot how to cook."

Celebrate!

71

➤ Romantic arithmetic: Champagne = Celebration.

➤ Today's homework: pick up a bottle of champagne on the way home from work . . . pop the cork with your lover . . . celebrate!

72

Buy a case of champagne. Label each bottle . . .

1. His birthday
2. Her birthday
3. Christmas
4. Your anniversary (of meeting or marrying)
5. For a midnight snack
6. Before making love
7. Celebrate a great accomplishment at work
8. The first snowfall
9. For making up after a fight
10. The first day of Spring

73

Balloons! Balloon bouquets. Helium-filled balloons. Heart-shaped red balloons. Mickey Mouse/Snoopy/Garfield balloons. Silvery, shiny balloons. Giant-sized balloons. Balloons with your names on them. Balloons with personalized messages on them. Check the Yellow Pages under . . . "Balloons".

➤ Celebrate all of the basics (birthdays,
anniversaries, holidays and Valentine's Day), and
then . . .
➤ Celebrate other special, crazy or unique occasions,
for instance:
  ➤ Beethoven's birthday (December 16)
  ➤ "Full Moon Day"
  ➤ The winter and summer Solstice
  ➤ Payday!

75

"Spontaneous Celebrations."

➤ Occasions: it's Tuesday! It's a sunny day!
Girlfriend Appreciation Day! Favourite Number
Day! Hug Day!
➤ Props: confetti. Champagne. Balloons. Pizza.
Candles. Chocolate.

76

Declare today "Couple's Day", "Wife Appreciation
Day", or some such nonsense. Use any excuse to go
out on the town tonight!

St. Valentine's Day

St. Valentine's Day is not the most romantic day of
the year. (You still have to recognize it and act on
it – but you don't get any extra credit for it, fellas.)
St. Valentine's Day is one of those *Obligatory
Romance* days.

77

Don't buy roses on Valentine's Day! It's common, expected and expensive.

- ❦ Buy *different* flowers.
- ❦ Or exercise your creativity: do something unique, quirky or touching.
- ❦ Write a poem . . . or copy one from a book of poetry.
- ❦ Write a love letter.

78

Turn Valentine's Day into a *real* holiday: take the day off work! Spend the day in bed. Go to the cinema. Go out to dinner. Go dancing. Take a drive. Make love. Go for a stroll.

79

Mail him a Valentine's Day card. Mail him 20! Make your own card. Make a *huge* card. Send a musical greeting card – available in most card shops.

Little Things Mean a Lot

80

Prescription for Romance #1: Compliment her. Repeat every four to six hours.

81

Prescription for Romance #2: Say "I love you" at least three times today. Repeat dosage every day for the rest of your life.

82

Write him a little love note; insert it in the book he's reading.

83

Prescription for Romance #3: Hug. Often!

84

Prescription for Romance #4: Run your hands under hot water before coming to bed(!)

85

Prescription for Romance #5: Create a flower bouquet.

86

Call her from work for no other reason than to tell her "I love you". Make it a habit.

87

Bring home her favourite:

- ◆ Ice cream
- ◆ Cookies
- ◆ Magazine
- ◆ Classic film on video
- ◆ Flower
- ◆ Chocolate

88

Prescription for Romance #6: Indulge your lover's hobby, sport or passion. Buy him a new golf club. Buy her a new tennis racket. Rent his favourite film. Get a gallon of her favourite ice cream.

Actions Speak Louder Than Words

89

Hug. Cuddle. Snuggle. Touch. Stroke.

90

Cuddle up in front of a roaring fire. (No TV. No kids. No phone.)

91

Leave a trail of your clothes, leading from the front door to your bedroom.

It's Not *What* You Do, But *How You Do It*

92

Don't just walk into the house tonight like you always do . . . Pause on the porch . . . ring the doorbell . . . and greet her with a rose and a bottle of champagne.

93

One woman in my Romance Class told us that her husband always manages to incorporate her favourite bear into his many gift presentations.

- ✦ He gave her diamond earrings by putting them on the bear's ears.
- ✦ He's strung pearls around the bear's neck.
- ✦ He's packed the bear inside boxes along with other gifts.
- ✦ He's put funny notes in the bear's paw.

94

Strings of pearls have been known to appear inside real clam shells at fancy restaurants.

95

Strings of pearls have also been presented to the tune of "A String of Pearls", by Glenn Miller.

And many diamond rings seem to find their way to the bottom of a glass of champagne.

97

Of course you know how to kiss, but perhaps a refresher course might add a little spark to your lives. Pick up a copy of a fun little book called *The Art of Kissing*, by William Kane. In it are instructions for (among other things) . . .

- ◆ The Candy Kiss
- ◆ The Sliding Kiss
- ◆ The Counter Kiss
- ◆ The Perfume Kiss
- ◆ The Japanese Kiss
- ◆ The Music Kiss
- ◆ The Surprise Kiss
- ◆ The Vacuum Kiss
- ◆ The French Kiss

98

Put a written message *inside* a balloon. If you can't find a clear balloon, use a regular one: insert the message, then attach a pin to the string.

The Way to a Man's Heart

The title of this chapter is a bit of a misnomer, as I've found that women are *at least* as food-orientated as men are. So we can safely say that one of the best ways to *anyone's* heart is through his or her stomach. *Bon appétit!*

99

You can spice up *any* meal at home – from gourmet extravaganzas to TV dinners – by adding candlelight and soft music. Don't wait for "special occasions" or for weekends, to bring out the romance.

100

Why not splurge, and hire a caterer to prepare a special meal *just for the two of you?* This way, you'll both have more time to relax, perhaps take a bubble bath together, and avoid dealing with pots and pans!

101

What's her all-time favourite meal? Learn to make it!

102

Create an "At-Home Date": includes dinner and dancing. Formal attire required.

103

For a sensual, silly time:

◆ Blindfold her.
◆ Sit her on the floor next to the refrigerator.
◆ Feed her a variety of delicious foods: strawberries, cherry tomatoes, cheese, ice cream, cookies, popcorn, yoghurt, watermelon, leftover chicken, pickles, olives, etc. (There's a great scene like this in the film *9¹/₂ Weeks.*)

104

Get the pizza chef to arrange the pepperoni in the shape of a heart.

105

Embark on a series of "Restaurant Discoveries": each week go to a different restaurant. Choose a restaurant "theme" that appeals to both of you, for instance:

◆ Find the best French restaurant in town.
◆ Mix-and-match all the ethnic restaurants: Chinese, Indian, Mexican, Greek, Thai, Italian, Japanese, etc.

106

Wine is the perfect complement to any nice meal. Find a wine you both enjoy. Buy a case of it and reserve it just for the two of you. Take a wine tasting course together.

Erotica

107

Let's start with the basics: do you *know* what your partner considers erotic? Or do you *assume* you know? Do you figure she likes what your last girlfriend enjoyed? Do you think he's just like the man described in last month's *Cosmo*?

✗ Talk about what each of you considers erotic.
✗ Set your inhibitions and judgements aside. (Maybe warm up with a little champagne.)
✗ Give yourselves plenty of time to explore this fun, complicated, frustrating-but-rewarding aspect of being human.

108

Go lingerie shopping together. (Accompany her into the dressing room.)

109

Get a copy of *The Joy of Sex*. Try some of its suggestions.

110

Kiss every square inch of her body . . . S-L-O-W-L-Y.

111

"Christen" every room in your house or flat by making love in it. (Don't forget to include the stairways and closets. The more adventurous among you may want to include the porches and back garden, too.)

112

Before you leave on a trip, leave a bottle of scented massage oil on the bedside table, along with a note saying "I'm going to use this entire bottle on you as soon as I return." (Then, keep your promise!)

113

End the day in a special way. Give her a massage.

Romance on a Budget

114

Where to get inexpensive flowers:

❋ Supermarkets ❋ Street vendors
❋ Your own garden

115

Timing is everything, when it comes to saving a few pounds. You could save 20% to 50% on virtually every gift you buy if you shop wisely . . .

❋ Hit the shops immediately after Christmas.
❋ Shop at end-of-the-season sales.
❋ Scan catalogues regularly, looking for deals.
❋ Go to holiday spots off-season.

116

Buy camping equipment instead of going on an expensive holiday. A one-time outlay will assure you of years of inexpensive holidays. (You'll also be prepared for last-minute holiday opportunities and quickie weekend get-aways.)

117

Many symphonies and theatres have discount tickets available on the day-of, or evening-of, performances.

If your partner doesn't mind a little uncertainty, this is a great way to save a few pounds and still enjoy an evening of culture and entertainment.

118

Buy *season tickets* instead of two-tickets-at-a-time for shows and events that you attend. You'll save money in the long run.

119

Buy wine and champagne by the case. You'll typically get a 10% to 20% discount off the per-bottle price. You'll save money, and always have a bottle on hand for those "Spontaneous Celebrations".

Spare No Expense

120

Maybe he'd like to fly on Concorde. A one-way ticket to America (New York) costs a little over £2,300.

121

And don't forget about:

- Caviare
- Antique fountain pens
- Diamond earrings, rings, and things
- 24-carat gold anything

122

You could update his entire album collection!
Convert his ageing album collection of beloved
Beatles albums, Moody Blues tunes and Rolling
Stones records to compact discs. Converting a
lifetime collection of some 500 albums would cost
around £6,000.

Basics

123

* Flowers
* Chocolate!
* The simple gold chain
* Greeting cards
  (shop-bought)
* Greeting cards
  (home-made)
* Jewellery
* Teddy bears
* Lingerie
* Love poems
* Love songs

124

* Love letters
* Surprises!
* "I love you" phone calls
* Romantic dinners in –
  at home by candle-light
* Sending flowers
  to the office
* Films in – with a video
* Singing "Your Song"
* Breakfast in bed
* Anniversary
  celebrations
* Weekend get-aways
* Romantic dinners out –
  at your favourite cosy
  restaurant
* Ballroom dancing
* Films out – to the
  cinema
* Walks on the beach

Bubble Baths

125

Start simple. Run her a bubble bath.

* Unless you already know her favourite type of bath powder, simply buy any.
* Note: A good steaming bath will stay hot for more than an hour. This gives you plenty of time to run it – leaving her alone to enjoy the surprise and a little privacy.

126

After you've gone through the basics a few times, choose a special evening and make a big production of it! Run the bath. Add candles. Garnish with cheese and fruit. Provide champagne. And a book to read. Then get rid of the kids, and make yourself scarce until it's time to towel her off.

127

Share a bubble bath.

128

Towel her dry after she showers.
S-L-O-W-L-Y.

129

A *wintertime* bath suggestion: *warm her towel in the dryer!* She'll adore you for at least a week afterwards.

130

Write her a love letter or poem. Roll it up and stick it in a bottle. Float the bottle in the bathtub.

131

(Baths aren't only for women!)

Creative Notes

132

Write her a note, poem or letter on one sheet of paper. Cut it up into puzzle-shaped pieces. Mail all the pieces to her in an envelope. Or . . . mail one puzzle piece a day for a week.

133

Write *I love you* on the bathroom mirror with a piece of soap.

134

❦ Draw funny faces on the eggs in the refrigerator.
❦ Get a local artist to draw a caricature of your smiling face on some eggs! (Look in the Yellow Pages under "Entertainment".)

135

Cut interesting/suggestive/unusual/funny headlines from the newspapers. When you've collected about

25 of them, simply put them in an envelope and mail them to your lover. The last batch I sent to my wife included these headlines:

- ❧ What's the Key to a Good Marriage? Good Sex
- ❧ Are We Cracking Under the Strain?
- ❧ Sex After Marriage?
- ❧ A perfect 10!
- ❧ Gifts Might Ease the Pain

136

Put notes/flowers/chocolates on his car windscreen.

137

Put notes on various household products:

- ❧ Anything by Old Spice: "You spice up my life!"
- ❧ Ritz Crackers: "Let's 'Put On The Ritz' tonight! Let's go dancing!"

Lame Excuses Department

138

Lame Excuse #1: "I don't have time". *Rubbish!* You have 1,440 minutes every day – the same as everybody else. How you use those minutes is up to you. If she doesn't rank up there with your work, your favourite sport and TV show, why don't you simply get a pet for companionship and save yourself the trouble of dealing with another human being?

139

Lame Excuse #2: "I forgot". That's okay. *Just don't do it again.* You're allowed to forget occasionally, but not consistently. If forgetting is a habit, you're sending a clear signal that she's just not that important to you. (If she's really *not* that important to you, why not be man enough to come right out and tell her, instead of making excuses?)

140

Lame Excuse #3: "Real Men aren't romantic". Who says so? Did you read it somewhere? Did your father tell you? Did you see it in a film? What do you really think, believe and feel when you're alone and being completely honest with yourself? When you're not trying to impress your mates, when you're not trying to bolster your self-esteem. If Real Men aren't romantic, then Real Men are *lonely*.

141

Lame Excuse #4: "Being romantic is going to cost me a fortune!" As the Beatles said, "Money can't buy me love". It's true. Money can buy you companionship, attention, sex and status – but it can't buy you love or happiness. Being romantic can cost you a fortune, but it doesn't have to. Don't confuse the size of the sentiment with the size of the price tag. If you do, you're in for a rude awakening some day.

Attitude Adjustment Section

142

Lower your inhibitions. Be spontaneous. Be silly. Be creative. Being a real romantic is a little like being slightly, enjoyably drunk. It lowers your inhibitions, causes you to act silly sometimes, and gives you the impetus to act impetuous.

143

Want to keep your marriage (or long-term relationship) fresh and vital? *Live as lovers.* Remember that that's how you started your relationship. You *can* recapture the *glow*, the passion and the excitement. It's largely a mindset, followed by a few active gestures. *Live as lovers.* Not just as husband and wife, mother and father, worker and housekeeper. First and foremost *you are lovers.*

144

Try being totally positive, accepting, supportive and non-judgmental for one entire week. No complaining, nagging, preaching, etc. It may change your life!

145

Do it without being asked. The unasked-for gesture is most appreciated. The surprise gift is most cherished. And, when you take the initiative, you feel a sense of accomplishment. (You've also given your partner the best encouragement for responding in kind.)

Kid's Stuff

146

Most women love soft toys.

147

Most men love gadgets, electronic stuff or tools . . .
"Boys' Toys". Men never really grow up – our toys
simply get more expensive.

148

When's the last time you watched cloud formations?
Take your lover for a walk in a field. Find an
unobstructed view. Flop down on a hilltop. What do
you see in the clouds? What do you imagine? (What
else might you two be able to do together in the
middle of a field??)

149

Notes with stuffed animals . . .

* Teddy bears: "I can't bear being away from
                    you . . ."
* Stuffed lions: "I'm roarin' to get you!"
* Stuffed tigers: "Grrrrrrr!"
* Stuffed monkeys: "Let's monkey around . . ."

150

Go fly a kite!

Love Is . . .

151

Love is . . . waking her gently with soft caresses and kisses.

152

Love is . . . eliminating all interruptions so you can *really* be alone together. Disconnect the phone; unplug the TV; ship the kids to the neighbours, disconnect the doorbell.

153

Love is . . . framing a favourite greeting card she's given you.

154

Love is . . . calling her from work to see if there's anything you can pick up for her on your way home.

155

Love is . . . reading aloud to each other before bed.

156

Love is . . . being there to greet her at the airport – *regardless of what time her flight arrives or how inconvenient it is for you.*

157

Love is . . . having a poem delivered to your table at a restaurant.

158

Love is . . . sending her a postcard every day that you're away from her.

I Love You

159

"I love you" (English)
"Nagligivaget" (Eskimo)
"Je t'aime" (French)
"Thaim in grabh leat" (Irish)
"Ai shite imasu" (Japanese)
"Ani ohev otakh" (Hebrew)
"Ich liebe dich" (German)
"Ya lyublyu tyebya"
   (Russian)

"Ti amo" (Italian)
"Te amo" (Spanish)
"Jag alskar dig"
   (Swedish)
"Aloha wau ia oe"
   (Hawaiian)
"Te quiero" (Mexican)
"Wo ai nei" (Chinese)
"S'agapo" (Greek)

160

Upside-down stamps on envelopes mean "I love you". (No, I didn't make this one up!! It's a tradition that was started during World War II, with soldiers and their lovers sending "secret love codes" to one another. This "code" caught on in a big way, and continues to this day.)

I'm In the Mood for Love

161

♥ Send her an "invitation": write that you're a researcher working on the new edition of *The Joy of Sex*, and you need her help with your studies.
♥ Send him an invitation: "Needed: An audience of one for an intimate Lingerie Fashion Show . . ."

162

Music sets the mood for love . . .

♥ Make custom tapes of romantic music.
♥ Find a good "soft jazz/New Age" radio station.
♥ Get a tape player with auto reverse, or a compact disc player, so you won't have to break the mood to change the record!

163

Some couples have created signals or gestures for use in *public*, all of which have essentially the same meaning . . .

♥ "I think I left the oven on. I'm afraid it's *getting hot* . . ."
♥ "Let's go home and watch TV."
♥ Hum "Your Song" in her ear.
♥ Scratch your left ear with your right hand.

164

Do you always make love at night? How about a little *afternoon delight?!*

165

Don't leave lovemaking until just before sleeping! Why is it so often the last item on the list? (Why do so many people have their priorities so screwed-up?? How could those silly household chores possibly be more important than being intimate with your lover?)

166

Drip honey on various parts of your lover's body. Lick it off. (Wine and cordials work nicely, too.)

Words of Love

167

"I love you". The all-purpose, over-used phrase . . . that we never tire of hearing. (When's the last time you told her?)

168

Memorize her favourite poem, or the lyrics to her favourite love song. Recite it at private times, or while making love.

169

- ♥ Write down the words to her favourite poem or love song, then post it to her.
- ♥ Write it on elegant parchment paper. Use a fountain pen.
- ♥ Have it rendered in beautiful calligraphy.
- ♥ Frame it!

170

Familiar words of love . . .

How do I love thee? Let me count the ways.
I love thee to the depth and breadth and height
My soul can reach, when feeling out of sight
For the ends of Being and ideal Grace
I love thee to the level of everyday's
Most quiet need, by sun and candle-light.
I love thee freely, as men strive for Right;
I love thee purely, as they turn from Praise.
I love thee with the passion put to use
In my old griefs, and with my childhood's faith.
I love thee with a love I seemed to lose
With my lost saints, – I love thee with the breath,
Smiles, tears, of all my life! – and, if God choose,
I shall but love thee better after death.

– Elizabeth Barrett Browning

171

Revive the lost art of writing love letters!

Do you feel silly trying to write a *love letter*? Do you think it's not cool to express your true/passionate/ insecure feelings? Maybe you'd feel more comfortable if you could see someone *else's* love letters, huh?

Here's one example that may give you encouragement (and perhaps some ideas):

♥ A letter from Napoleon Bonaparte to Josephine De Beauharnais:

"I wake filled with thoughts of you. Your portrait and the intoxicating evening which we spent yesterday have left my senses in turmoil. Sweet, incomparable Josephine, what a strange effect you have on my heart!"

♥ A whole *bookful* of passionate outpourings is available in *Love Letters*, edited by Antonia Fraser.

Rituals of Romance

173

Rituals can be elaborate, serious and meaningful. Or they can be fun, silly and quirky. They can be personal, private and secret, or public and shared.

174

Some couples have *morning* rituals:

- ♣ They spend ten minutes talking in bed before rising.
- ♣ They read an affirmation aloud to one another.
- ♣ They make a point of kissing before parting.

175

Some couples have *evening* rituals:

- ♣ They go for a walk after dinner together.
- ♣ They meditate silently together.
- ♣ They take turns every other night giving each other backrubs.

176

And, there are Sunday morning rituals:

- ♣ Attending a church service together.
- ♣ Reading the Sunday papers aloud to each other.
- ♣ Sunday brunch.

Do's and Don'ts

177

Don't buy a dozen red roses on Valentine's Day. It's common, it's expected, and it's expensive. Instead, buy a Bonsai tree for her, or choose flowers that match her eyes.

178

Don't buy practical items for gifts. Appliances are wonderful, but *don't give them as gifts!* (My father-in-law learned his lesson the hard way. For their first Christmas today, he gave his wife . . . an electric broom. To put it mildly, she was not pleased.)

Exceptions: ☆ Gourmet kitchen utensils (for the fanatical chef).

☆ Tools (for some men).

179

Contrary to popular belief, you should not use romance to apologise after a fight! If you do, you'll taint *all* your romantic gestures for a long time to come. (After a fight, a simple, sincere apology is best. Resume romantic gestures *after* you've both cooled down, or after a week – whichever is later.)

180

Know your anniversaries. All of them . . .

☆ Your wedding
☆ The day you first met
☆ Your first date
☆ Your first kiss
☆ Your first . . .
☆ The first time you made love

☆ Your first big blow-out fight
☆ The day you moved in together
☆ The day you bought your home
☆ The first time you said "I love you"

Fun and Games

181

Go to a carnival, fair or amusement park together.
(Without the children.)

182

Go for a walk.

- ☆ Directions: Find the nearest beach, forest or park.
- ☆ Instructions: Stand side-by-side. Hold hands. Walk. Talk.

183

Ladies, fulfil a fantasy: arrange a surprise ski weekend; give him a backrub; greet him at the door with just a smile . . .

184

Guys, fulfil a fantasy: run a bubble bath for her; cook dinner; rent her favourite film; make love *the way she wants to be made love to.*

185

Check your local Yellow Pages, under "Costumes: Fancy Dress." And then . . .

- ☆ Rent a costume, surprise her! Be a cowboy, doctor, policeman, mechanic, caveman, astronaut.
- ☆ Rent a costume, surprise *him!* Be a ballerina, policewoman, doctor, girl guide, classy callgirl, elf.

186

Go on a "Trinket Gift Hunt". Here's how it works: you each get £10 and 30 minutes to shop for each other. The goal is to buy as many different fun/crazy/significant/silly "Trinket Gifts" as possible, for your partner.

Weird and Wacky

187

Greet him at the door with confetti.

188

Giftwrap a wishbone in a jewellery box. Send it to her with a note that says, "I wish you were here".

189

Kidnap her! Blindfold her; drive her around town until she's definitely lost; then reveal your destination: her favourite restaurant, or maybe a romantic inn!

Romantics Are . . .

190

Romantics are flexible.

✹ Decide on the spur of the moment to take a half day off work!

* Consciously "change gears" at the end of the day – from your "business mode" into your "personal mode". Most working people need to practise turning their feelings back on at the end of the day.

191

Romantics have a good sense of humour. There's no such thing as a "humourless romantic". While the *foundation* of romance is a serious love, the *nature* of romance is lighthearted.

192

Romantics are passionate. I'm not talking about sexual passion here, but about a passion for *life*. Romantics don't allow their lives, or love lives, to slide into boredom – the deadly enemy of all relationships.

193

Romantics "work at it" – and "play at it", too! Being a romantic is not the same as being a starry-eyed, unrealistic dreamer. Romantics often work long and hard to pull off some of their "romantic masterpieces". Romantics plan and scheme, buy gifts ahead of time, search for sales, and stock up on greeting cards. And, of course, romantics play and have a lot of fun.

194

Romantics are always "dating". Familiarity breeds contempt *only if you let it*! There are *thousands* of ways to keep your relationship fresh and new.

195

Romantics live in the moment.

"Carpe diem" – *seize the day*! Don't put it off until tomorrow! Do something passionate for your lover. Do it now! Do it with feeling!

* Do something unexpected for your lover *today!*
* Do something totally outrageous.
* Do something totally out of character for you – surprise her!
* Do something sexy.
* Do something sensitive.
* Do something creative.

The Gospel According to Godek

196

Romantic gestures have no ulterior motive. Their only purpose is to express love and appreciation, to show that you've been thinking of your partner.

197

* Romance is an art, not a science: you can't predict

it or "get it" perfectly. So you logical, "left-brained" folks are going to have to loosen up, let go and get creative!

* Romance is not a sport. It's not a competition. No points are awarded.
* Romance is not a business. There's no bottom line.

198

Romance is a state of mind, an attitude. It's not so much *what* you do as *how you do it.* This is why little gestures work so well. It's also why some people (mostly men) just don't "get it" when it comes to romance. If you approach romance and relationships with a cynical attitude – or a rigid, overly-practical state of mind – you just won't tune in to what's going on here.

199

* The highest form of romance is *optional romance* – gestures made that are not required or expected.
* The middle form – *obligatory romance* – is that which is required by custom or culture. It's important, but of minor consequence in the larger scheme of keeping relationships functioning at a high level of passion.
* The lowest form – *reluctant romance* – is hardly worth mentioning. It's dishonest on the part of the giver, and an insult to the recipient.

200

Romance doesn't equal love. It's the *expression* of love; the language of love is; the real-world expression of an ideal.

Satin and Lace

201

Ladies: if you remember only *one thing* from this book, remember this: men *love* lingerie. Hundreds of men in the Romance Class have confided or complained that having their ladies wear more lingerie is the one thing they want intensely that their women tend to hold back on.

202

Gentlemen: approach the subject *gently*.

- Your first lingerie present should *not* be a peek-a-boo bra.
- You might start by giving her a say in the matter: attach a £20 note to a lingerie catalogue with a note saying "You choose". Or custom-make a "Lingerie Coupon".

Love Coupon

Nightgowns! Teddies!! Stockings!!! Suspenders!!!!

This coupon is good for a £50 shopping spree in the
nearest lingerie store or lingerie catalogue.

A gift to: ....

A gift from: ....

Le Boudoir

203

The bedroom is your *private, romantic hide-away.*
Don't turn it into an all-purpose room.

➵ Get rid of that TV!   ➵ No exercise equipment.
➵ No bright lights.   ➵ Massage oil is a must.

204

Don't simply have breakfast in bed – make it an
elegant feast. Use your good china and crystal. Add
candles and flowers.

205

Breakfast in bed is nice – but rather *common*, don't
you think? How about *dinner* in bed!

206

The True Test of Love and Tolerance, #1: Let her warm her cold feet on you in bed.

207

➻ Leave a rose on her pillow.
➻ Leave a note on his pillow.
➻ Lay out the lingerie outfit you'd like her to wear.
➻ Spread rose petals all over the bedroom.

For Men Only

208

A shopping trip for men. Buy one item from each store. Giftwrap in separate boxes and give!

➤ Crabtree & Evelyn
➤ Hallmark Card shop
➤ A local flower shop
➤ A quality jewellery shop

209

Another shopping trip for men. Pick up all those items in coordinated fragrances: body lotion, hand lotion, shampoo, conditioner, bath gel, perfumed soap, etc. She'll love you for it. Guaranteed.

210

Do a household chore that's usually one of "her" jobs:

➤ Cook dinner
➤ Clean the bathroom
➤ Do the grocery shopping
➤ Take the kids to football practice

211

Do something *with* her that you hate to do (and do it cheerfully without complaint): go clothes shopping with her; go out to the cinema with her; attend the ballet with her; do some gardening with her.

212

Do something *for* her that you hate doing: go grocery shopping, weed the garden, get up in the middle of the night for the baby.

213

Buy her an entire outfit. Include: beautiful lingerie, a gorgeous dress, a matching scarf, pin or necklace, and shoes! Spread 'em out on the bed. Wait for her jaw to drop.

214

Listen to her! Don't problem-solve; don't give advice; don't agree or disagree. Just *listen*. Validate her. Often, when men think women are looking for *answers*, they're simply looking for *compassion and understanding*! (This is one of those sex-based differences: men tend to be orientated around problem-solving; women around relationships.)

For Women Only

215

Send him a letter sealed with a kiss. (Use your reddest lipstick.)

216

Send him a *perfumed* love letter.

217

Don't position yourself against his passions. Don't force him to choose between you and his golf/football/cricket/cars/fishing! As they say, "If you can't beat 'em, join 'em!" Read a book about his favourite sport/hobby/pastime so you can join in, or at least understand what's going on.

218

Send him flowers at work.

219

Do something *with* him that you hate to do (and do it cheerfully and without complaint). Go fishing, bowling, birdwatching, running or camping with him; watch "The Game" on TV.

220

Do something *for* him that you hate doing. Iron his shirts; wash his car; cook his favourite hard-to-make dinner; run some errands; cut the lawn.

For Singles Only

221

Mail her a copy of your résumé instead of a greeting card. Attach a note: "I'd like you to get to know me better."

222

Romantic Strategy #1 for Cleverly Meeting Someone at Work: send a dozen pink roses to her anonymously; then place one pink rose on your desk, where she's sure to notice it. (You take it from there . . .)

223

➤ If you've talked about possibly moving in together, and you decide you want to go for it, wrap your flat key in a gift box and give it to her.

➤ Or – mail it to her with a note: "You've got the key to my heart . . . now I want you to have *this* key."

For Marrieds Only

224

"Re-frame" your relationship:

➢ She's not your wife – she's your *lover*.
➢ He's not your husband – he's that handsome devil
  that you fell head-over-heels in love with,
  remember?!

225

➢ Go on a second honeymoon.
➢ Go on a third honeymoon.

226

Save your "Just Married" sign (or make a new one).
Tape it to the back windscreen of your car before
taking a Sunday afternoon drive. People will honk
and wave . . . you'll feel like a newly-wed again!

227

Revisit the place where you proposed marriage. Take
along a bottle of champagne. Reminisce!

228

"Recommended" wedding anniversary gifts. (Just
who made up this list, anyway??)

Year	Traditional	Modern
1	Cotton	Clocks
2	Paper	China

3	Leather	Crystal/glass
4	Fruit/flowers	Appliances
5	Wood	Silver/silverware
6	Iron	Wood
7	Wool	Desk sets
8	Bronze	Linens/laces
9	Pottery/Copper	Leather
10	Tin	Diamond jewellery
11	Steel	Fashion jewellery
12	Silk/linen	Pearls
13	Lace	Textiles/furs
14	Ivory	Gold jewellery
15	Crystal	Watches
20	China	Platinum
25	Silver	Silver
30	Pearl	Diamond or pearl
35	Coral	Jade
40	Ruby	Ruby
45	Sapphire	Sapphire
50	Gold	Gold
55	Emerald	Emerald
60	Diamond	Diamond

Married . . . With Children

229

Instead of having the babysitter come in while you go out, *have the babysitter take the kids out – while you two stay home!* Send all of them to the cinema – a double feature. ("Now, what was it we used to do with all this peace and quiet? Oh, yes . . .!")

230

Men: add Mother's Day to your list of *Obligatory Romance* dates to observe. Mark it on your calendar *now*.

231

Make special "Love Coupons" to help each other deal with the children:

➤ An "I'll get up in the middle of the night for the baby" coupon.
➤ An "It's my turn to stay home with the next sick child" coupon.
➤ A coupon for "Five 'taxi trips': driving the children to football practice."
➤ An "I'll cook the kids' dinner" coupon.

Engaging Ideas

232

Apply for the job of "Husband"!

▶ Write a "Personal Résumé" outlining your desirable qualities, your qualifications and relevant experience. Write an appropriate cover letter, and mail it to her or present it in person.
▶ You may want to send a copy to her parents! (Then again, maybe not!)

233

One man in the Romance Class was inspired to present his girlfriend with one red rose . . . which had a diamond ring hidden inside the unopened bud. The rose sat on her desk for two days, where she admired it and smelled it often, before it bloomed, revealing the ring!

234

Why should women be the only ones to get engagement rings??

235

Here are some of the more creative and unusual ways that people have got engaged:

- Sky banner proposals
- Custom jigsaw puzzle proposals
- Proposals inside custom-made Chinese fortune cookies
- Proposals on billboards
- Videotaped proposals
- Audiotaped proposals
- Telegrammed proposals
- Using lit candles to spell out "Will you marry me?"
- Painting the proposal on the roof, then taking her flying!

Making Beautiful Music Together

236

Choose your favourite songs (and your lover's!), and create cassette tapes of romantic background music. (While you're at it, make *several* tapes.)

237

Create a custom tape of meaningful/romantic love songs for her!

☞ Choose about ten great songs, and record them on a cassette tape.

☞ Don't just *hand* the darn thing to her – give it to her in a Walkman, or insert it in her car tape player with a little note attached!

Communicating

238

Listen, for a change. You'll learn a lot about your partner.

☞ Listen for the feelings behind the words. We don't always say what we mean, but the emotional content is still there if we tune in to it.

☞ Listen without interrupting. (Quite a challenge – especially if you've been together for many years!)

239

Give your partner more reassurance. Reinforce her good qualities. Compliment his talents and abilities. Reinforce all the good qualities *that attracted you to your partner in the first place.*

☞ Tell him what you really appreciate about him.
☞ Remind her that you really do adore her.
☞ Concentrate on the positive when talking to him.
☞ Focus on who she *really is,* instead of on your unrealistic fantasy of "The Perfect Woman".

240

Here are some guidelines for Courtship Conversation:

☞ Talk to one another with respect.
☞ Remember that conversation involves two-way communication.
☞ Complete honesty is demanded, assumed, and never questioned.
☞ Speak from the heart, but don't leave the head behind.
☞ Maintain eye contact.

Togetherness

241

Read the Sunday newspaper in bed together.

242

☞ Go cycling together.
☞ Rent a bicycle built for two!

243

Buy a guide book for the city or region where you live. Visit somewhere you've never been before.

244

Explore together: auctions, flea markets, secondhand stores, garage sales and jumble sales. They're great places to find "Trinket Gifts" as well as practical things you just might need around the house.

245

Plant and care for a garden together. Crawling around in the dirt together has a funny way of bringing a couple closer.

246

Cook a meal together.

247

Eat dinner by candle-light. Heck – eat breakfast by candle-light!

248

Go into a bookstore together. Buy each other two books.

☞ One that you know your partner will like . . .
☞ And one that you want your partner to read.

249

Take lessons together.

☞ Wine tasting	☞ Golfing	☞ Yoga
☞ Windsurfing	☞ Guitar	☞ Cooking
☞ Hang-gliding!	☞ Dancing	☞ Sailing

At Home

250

Your home should never be without flowers. They add an elegant touch to your living room or den; they brighten up your kitchen; and they serve as a living (and aromatic) reminder of your love for one another.

251

Don't wait till Saturday night to go out dancing. Dance by yourselves at home in your living room.

252

Wash her hair for her. She'll love it. Guaranteed.

253

Carry her over the threshold of your house or flat.
(Not for newly-weds only!)

Around Town

254

Around your town are all the shops you'll need to inspire and satisfy your romantic urges. Try browsing in each of these types of shops with nothing specifically in mind . . . and see what romantic possibilities jump out at you:

- Book shops
- Sport shops
- Card shops
- Music shops
- Boutiques
- Lingerie shops
- Video shops
- Toy shops
- Secondhand shops

255

Go for a "mystery drive" in the country. Keep to the back roads and ignore the map. Agree to have lunch at the first charming inn you pass.

- If you stumble onto a quaint bed-and-breakfast, stay the night!
- If you keep your camping equipment in the boot, you'll be ready for all kinds of opportunities.

256

Check out the adult education programmes in your area. Most programmes include many one-session seminars and workshops that are fun and entertaining as well as educational.

♣ Attend a class *together*: Dancing, massage, yoga, exercise, cooking . . .
♣ . . . Or sign him up for a class you know he'll enjoy.

Dining Out

257

Did you know that there are *two* kinds of romantic restaurants?

1. **The elegant/active/often-with-great-views restaurant**
2. **The small/dark/cosy-with-tiny-tables restaurant**

Which kind of restaurant does she prefer? Don't take her to *one* when she's crazy about the *other*.

258

♣ Arrange to have a small gift delivered to your table just before the main course is served.
♣ Arrange to have a dozen red roses delivered to your table.
♣ Hire a musician to serenade your lover at your table.

259

Get a menu from his favourite restaurant. Turn it into a "Certificate Good for One Romantic Dinner". Mail it to him at work.

260

A checklist of different *types* of restaurants to experience together:

- Indian
- Chinese
- French
- Greek
- Vegetarian
- Italian
- Japanese
- Mexican
- Steak
- Thai
- Vietnamese
- Seafood

261

Have lunch or dinner in an unusual place. Many museums have nice cafés. Or how about dinner at the airport? Outdoor cafés?

262

Get up extra early on a weekday and go out for breakfast with your lover. It's a great way to start the day in a totally different way.

263

Sunday brunch! Ask your friends for their favourite spots.

Off the Wall

264

Fake a power cut at home. (Loosen the fuses or throw the breaker switches.) Get out the candles. Then try to think of *something* to do . . .

265

Test drive a Porsche together.

266

Write wacky notes, memos and things, based on
your profession:

- ✔ Teacher: Write a report card.
- ✔ Lawyer: Write out a summons.
- ✔ Traffic Warden: Write her a ticket.
- ✔ Doctor: Write a prescription.
- ✔ Secretary: Write a memo.
- ✔ Salesman: Place an order.
- ✔ Van driver: Write a packing slip.
- ✔ Anyone: Write a personal résumé.

267

Write her a cheque for a million kisses.

268

Slow dance at a restaurant – *when there's no music
playing.*

No-Cost Gestures

269

Go wild in the kitchen! (And after you do that, cook
her favourite meal for her!)

270

When's the last time you took a moonlit stroll?

271

Unplug the TV. Put a note on the screen saying
"Turn me on instead".

Potpourri

272

Picnics! (I have checked, and nowhere is it written
that you can't have picnics indoors, in the nude, in
front of a fireplace, in your office, in bed, on the roof
of your apartment building, or at midnight.)

273

Go through revolving doors together.

274

Keep candles in the car. Eat dinner by candle-light
the next time you go to McDonald's.

What's In a Name?

275

Do you know the *significance* of your lover's name?
Here are a few samples taken from a "baby name"
book:

- **Ada** is "joyous".
- **Amy** is "beloved", from the Latin.
- **Barbara** means "mysterious stranger".
- **Cathleens** and **Kathys** are "pure".
- **Diane** derives from the Latin Diana, meaning "Goddess of the Moon".
- **Gary** is a "mighty spear".
- **Gregory** is a "vigilant".
- **Jean, Janet** and **Joanna** are all variations of John . . .
- **John** is "God's gracious gift".
- **Judy** is "admired and praised".
- **Kevin** is "kind and gentle".
- **Linda** is Spanish, meaning "beautiful".
- **Marys** and **Maureens** are either a "wished-for child", or "rebellious".
- **Monica** is an "advisor".
- **Tracey** is a modern version of **Teresa**, meaning "reaper".
- **Warren** is a "defender".
- **Wendy** was invented by J.M. Barrie for the heroine of Peter Pan!

276

If her name is April, May or June, declare the corresponding month "her" month, and do something special for her every day. (Every woman is "one-in-a-million", but few are "one-in-twelve"!)

277

Name your boat after her.

Guidelines

278

Timing. Timing is *everything*.

↦ Belated birthday cards ought to be outlawed.

↦ Chocolate is romantic – *but not if she's on a diet.*

↦ Stick to *small* romantic gestures when he's totally preoccupied with a big work project. (Save the biggies until he can appreciate them.)

↦ Pulling surprises requires a superb sense of timing.

279

Dot your *i's* and cross your *t's.* In other words, pay attention to details!

↦ Don't buy just *any* flowers – get her favourites.

↦ Make a point of *always* wrapping his gifts in his favourite colour.

↦ Don't buy her *gold* jewellery when she prefers *silver.*

280

"Walk a mile in his shoes," then re-think your romantic gestures.

↦ After an especially tough week, he'd probably prefer a massage to going out to the cinema.

↦ Don't bring her flowers when what she *really* needs is two hours of peace and quiet. (Two hours of peace and quiet just may be the best gift you ever give her!)

281

Romantics are not martyrs! They don't put their partners first by ignoring their own needs and wants. Rather, they put their relationship first, and do things that enhance the couple as a whole. Self-sacrifice always backfires because it builds resentment in the giver and creates guilt in the receiver. Romantic gestures performed out of love provide benefits to both the giver and the receiver.

Resources

282

Brides magazines are great resources for finding romantic vacation destinations. (If you think honeymoons are just for newly-weds, you're missing some great romantic opportunities!)

283

Resources around town. Call 'em! Ask 'em questions! Send for their catalogues and brochures!

- ➡ Adult education programmes
- ➡ Local Tourist Board
- ➡ Golf courses
- ➡ Tennis clubs

284

Consult these resources:

- Yellow Pages
- Your local newspaper
- The public library
- Daily newspaper
- Popular magazines
- Catalogues

285

FLOWERS – various resources:

- Supermarkets
- Street vendors
- Your garden
- Look in Yellow Pages for your nearest florist.

Mementos

286

Have you saved any old love letters you've sent to each other? Dust them off and re-read them. Maybe read them aloud to each other. Revive the memories; re-experience your love as it was when it was new.

287

Stuff to save:

- Cinema tickets, theatre programmes, restaurant receipts.
- Sand and seashells from your beach vacations.
- Labels from wine bottles and corks from champagne bottles.
- Restaurant menus and placements.

288

Page through your photo albums together on a rainy afternoon.

The Golden Rules of Romance

289

The receiver defines what's romantic.

- ❤ If you give her flowers, and she hates flowers, it isn't romantic.
- ❤ If you've spent all day cooking a gourmet meal, and he'd rather call for a pizza . . . guess what?
- ❤ If you've spent a fortune on an outfit for her, and she says it isn't her style, you have no right to be resentful.

290

Time and effort expended are usually more appreciated than money spent.

291

Romantic gestures have no ulterior motive.

Their only purpose is to express love; to show that she's important and special to you; to let him know you think about him often.

292

Planning doesn't destroy spontaneity – it creates opportunity.

293

❤ The unasked-for gift is most appreciated.

❤ The surprise gift is most cherished

294

The Romantic Law of Inverse Proportions:

❤ *The more you need romance in your life, the less likely you are to do it; the less you need it, the more likely you are to do it.*

Gift Ideas

295

Get her something that she's always wanted to have, but always held back on . . . because it was too expensive, too impractical, too weird or too self-indulgent.

296

Music boxes!

297

Buy her some romantic reading . . . *Mills & Boon* and *Silhouette* offer beautifully packaged short story collections and gift packs.

298

Doesn't he deserve a trophy for being the "World's Best Lover"? Doesn't she merit a loving cup to celebrate her latest accomplishment? Trophy shops have a wealth of ideas waiting for you: plaques, medals, rosettes, nameplates, certificates and banners. And they're all personalized, engraved, lettered or monogrammed. Check the Yellow Pages under "Trophies"!

299

Get gift items to go along with your pet names for each other:

✔ Babe
✔ Big Bear
✔ Bunny
✔ Cookie
✔ Cupcake
✔ Fuzzy
✔ Gumdrop

✔ Honey bun
✔ Jellybean
✔ Kitten
✔ Lover
✔ Macho Man
✔ Muffin

✔ Peeper
✔ Piglet
✔ Playmate
✔ Pussycat
✔ Sweetie
✔ Teddy bear
✔ Tiger

300

Don't forget about charm bracelets! They bring good memories alive, and they provide a built-in gift idea for any occasion.

301

Best and Worst Gifts: ✔ Best: the gift of time.

✔ Worst: practical gifts.

The Gift of Time

302

The gift of time:

- ✔ Two hours of peace and quiet
- ✔ A day without the children
- ✔ A weekend get-away
- ✔ A little "afternoon delight"

303

"Double-up" on activities. Combine various activities and you'll find more time to be together:

- ✔ Meet for lunch. (You have to eat anyway, right?!)
- ✔ Eat dinner and watch a romantic film on video.
- ✔ Do a chore together: go grocery shopping, take the car to the shop.

304

Practise "chore-shifting". Don't go grocery shopping on *Friday night*! Don't do laundry on *Saturday morning*! Those are valuable times – times you could be spending *together*.

✔ Find ways to shift chores to more efficient times.
✔ Do two chores at the same time.
✔ Do chores together: doubling the person power more than doubles the efficiency!

305

✔ You can *save* time by shopping via catalogue.
✔ You can *reorganize* time by "chore-shifting".
✔ You can *create* time by "doubling up" on activities.
✔ You can *use time more efficiently* by buying a book on time management.
✔ You can *release* time by hiring a housecleaning service.
✔ You can *find* time by planning better.

306

Make time in the morning to make love. Get up an hour early!

Break Out of That Rot!

307

Do something *totally out of character.*

✦ Always late? Be on time.
✦ Not creative? Write a blockbuster.
✦ Forgetful? Remember her birthday *every day for a month!*

✦ Watch TV every night? Go out to dinner instead.

308

Act out different fantasies of meeting for the first time.

✦ Meet in a bar after work.
✦ Meet while grocery shopping.
✦ Meet in a queue, waiting at the bank.
✦ Meet over lunch at work.

309

A *quickie vacation* is a great way to "break out of the rot". Call your local travel agent. Find out what last-minute specials are available, what kinds of discount tickets are being offered, which hotels are running special promotions, and which destinations are hot!

310

If you're especially inept in the kitchen you've got a great opportunity to surprise your partner. *Cook a gourmet meal*! Send your partner out for the afternoon. Enlist the help of a friend who cooks. Prepare your lover's favourite dish. *Voilá!*

311

Spend an "all-nighter" together: make love, watch videos, go for a moonlit stroll, make love again, watch old films on TV, blast the stereo and dance at 3.00 a.m. Then sleep all day the next day.

Memorize This List!

312

Know your lover's favourite things. Compile a list of items such as:

- ✦ Colour
- ✦ Singer
- ✦ Chocolate
- ✦ Musical
- ✦ Drink
- ✦ Flower
- ✦ Music
- ✦ Restaurant
- ✦ Sport
- ✦ Food
- ✦ Author
- ✦ Magazine
- ✦ Film
- ✦ Hobby

313–321

- ✦ Visit a museum gift shop for a poster print by her favourite artist.
- ✦ Get the whole "family of products" in the fragrance of her favourite perfume (bath salts, soaps, body lotions, candles, etc.).
- ✦ Get a first edition book signed by his favourite author.
- ✦ Get every recording ever made by his favourite musical group.
- ✦ Buy her every book ever written by her favourite author.
- ✦ Wrap all her gifts in her favourite colour.
- ✦ Get the book of *Love Signs*, by Linda Goodman. It contains astrological descriptions of every possible pairing of the 12 Signs of the Zodiac!

✦ Get a set of comedy videos that you know will really crack him up: Monty Python, Robin Williams, Black Adder.

✦ Buy three ties for him: one business tie, one casual tie, and one truly outrageous tie.

Go Away!

322

Go on a cruise! Take your lover and experience "The Love Boat" for yourself.

323

Before going on vacation, get piles of brochures, posters and books about your upcoming destination. Send them to him in a constant and varied stream of mail.

324

Tour a vineyard.

Movie Madness

325

Hold an At-Home Video Film Festival! Rent the videos, pop the popcorn, clear the calendar, and roll!

☆ Some romantic favourites:
- An Officer and a Gentleman
- Casablanca
- On Golden Pond
- Funny Girl
- Ghost
- Gone with the Wind
- Out of Africa
- Romeo and Juliet
- From Here to Eternity
- The French Lieutenant's Woman
- West Side Story
- When Harry Met Sally
- Love Story

☆ Some erotic favourites:
- $9^1/_2$ Weeks
- Dangerous Liaisons
- Sea of Love
- The Fabulous Baker Boys

326

Your At-Home Video Film Festival could revolve around favourite film stars.

327

Or, create "themes" for your At-Home Video Film Festivals. Choose your lover's favourite "type" or genre of film:

☆ Comedy
☆ Science fiction
☆ The James Bond films
☆ All the Beatles' films
☆ All of Woody Allen's films
☆ All the Pink Panther films

Do It Outside

328

Watch the sunset together. Find a hill. Bring a picnic. It's better than TV!

329

In the winter, warm up her car for her! And while you're at it, brush the snow off her windscreen, too.

330

Go camping! Borrow friends' equipment for starters. If you enjoy it, buy your own stuff. (Make sure you include a double sleeping bag on your equipment list.)

331

When's the last time you played miniature golf or pitch and putt? Match your skills and have a good time.

332

Go hiking. Go to a football match. Go to a Royal Park. Go to an outdoor public garden. Go to an outdoor classical concert. Go on a picnic. Go for a ride in the country. Go for a walk. Go for it!

Do It In Public

333

* Do you praise her in public? Complimenting her in front of someone else will make her feel extra special.
* When's the last time you told someone else how lucky you feel to have this woman in your life?

334

Do you remember what teenagers used to call "PDAs" – Public Displays of Affection? Are you out of the habit of showing affection for your partner in public? Hold hands. Rest your hand on his shoulder. Entwine your arm with hers.

335

Flirt with her at a party, as if you both were single.

* For beginners: flirt just a little. Wink. Compliment her.
* For intermediate students: act out a complete "pick-up" fantasy, without any of the other guests being aware of what you are doing.
* For advance students: continue the fantasy as you return home!

336

Place an ad in the Personal Column of your local newspaper. Let your lover know why he or she is so special. Write it in "code", possibly using your private pet name for her. This is a great opportunity to exercise your creativity and express your feelings in just a few clever words.

✳ When your ad appears, circle it and leave it on the kitchen table when you leave for work.
✳ Or call him at work on the day the ad appears, and tell him there's a secret message for him on page such-and-such.

Do-It-Yourself

337

✳ Write a song ✳ Pen a poem
✳ Write a love letter ✳ Jot a love note

338

Write your own version of Elizabeth Barrett Browning's famous poem . . . *"How do I love thee, let me count the ways . . ."*

339

✳ Make custom cassette tapes of romantic background music.
✳ Make custom tapes of meaningful, romantic songs as gifts for her.

340

Make a custom banner to welcome him home from a trip – or just to say *"I love you!"*

341

Learn to do *calligraphy*. You'll add a touch of class
to even the simplest note.

Shopping Strategies

342

Try shopping in museum gift shops. They tend to
have a unique, classy and/or unusual collection of
items:

* For a touch of class, try art museums.
* For scientific and technical stuff, try science
  museums.
* For spacey stuff, try planetariums.
* For interesting mementos, try historic museums.

343

When window shopping together, pay close
attention for items that she really likes. Sneak back
later and get them for her.

344

Catalogues! Send for them! Keep them in a basket in
the bathroom! Scan through them occasionally! Note
the great gift ideas!

Travel Tips

345

When she's going away by herself, give her a "Trip Survival Kit". (It would be nice to package it in a gift box or fancy bag – but you don't have to.)

Anyway . . . now fill the Kit with stuff.

346

Arrange with an airline stewardess to have a gift or flower delivered to her after her flight is airborne.

347

* Pack a card inside his suitcase. Pack 10!
* Hide little "love notes" everywhere: in his socks and shoes and shirt pockets and suit pockets and briefcase and suitcase and wallet and notebooks and files and . . .
* Pack his favourite chocolates.

348

Give him a custom-made tape in a Walkman just before he goes on a business trip. Tell him he can't play it until the plane is airborne.

349

Mail a card or note to her on the day you leave town, so she'll get it while you're away.

350

Send a greeting card to her hotel, so it's waiting for her when she arrives.

Give It a Twist

351

A basic romantic concept: birthday cards. Some twists:

* Send a card a day for a week, a month.
* Send as many cards as the number of years in his age.
* Hide cards in his briefcase, in the refrigerator.
* Create your own birthday cards.
* Write a personal birthday message on a private part of your body . . . and let him discover it.
* Write a birthday greeting on a cake – or on a pizza.

352

A basic romantic concept: create your own "Love Coupons" – and use 'em!

Some twists:

* Backrub coupons
* Music Tape coupons
* Lovemaking coupons
* Picnic coupons
* Romantic Dinner (Out or In) coupons
* "I'll Do Your Chores" coupons

* A Ride in the Country coupons
* An Evening of Dancing coupons

Love Coupon

This coupon entitles the holder to one
candlelit dinner . . .
(with the issuer of the coupon)
at the most romantic restaurant in town!

A gift to: ....

A gift from: ....

353

Basic romantic concept: love letters, love notes,
poetry and verses. Some twists:

* Turn them into scrolls, tied with ribbon.
* Frame 'em.
* Place a love note in the Classified section of the
  newspaper.
* Create a poster.
* Write a letter in code.

Picture This!

354

Have a special photograph blown up to poster size!

355

* You do, of course, carry a photo of her in your wallet, *don't you*?
* And you have an 8-by-10 of her on your desk at work, *right*??

356

Find some old photos of yourself, or go through your photo album. Add funny captions. Mail them to her.

Let's Get Physical!

357

There's a big difference between a *sensual* massage and a *sexual* message. One relaxes the recipient, and may lull your lover to sleep. The other stimulates the recipient, and will turn your lover into a lover!

358

Take a massage class together.

359

Go skinny-dipping: in the ocean, in a pond or lake, in your pool, in the neighbour's pool!

360

Make love in other unusual places, too: cars, trains, beaches, pools, boats, ponds/lakes/ocean, store dressing rooms, libraries, lifts, bathtubs, fire escapes, porches, rooftops, sauna and hot tubs.

Miscellany

361

Musical greeting cards!

362

A gift-a-day for the 12 Days of Christmas!

363

Everyone should, at one time or another in his or her life:

➤ Go skinny-dipping
➤ Take a moonlit stroll on a beach
➤ Stay up all night talking and making love
➤ Go gambling in Las Vegas
➤ Get giddy on champagne

364

➤ Keep this book handy – don't stick it up on your bookshelf! Carry it around in your briefcase, keep it next to the TV *Guide*; skim through it occasionally.

➤ Make a habit of using this book to enhance your love life! Circle ideas you know (or suspect) your lover will love.

365

Enjoy yourself

EXPRESS YOURSELF

Reveal yourself

Share Yourself

Know thyself

Love yourself

Develop yourself

Risk yourself

Be yOuRself

Give yourself!